**FROM THE LEAST SELLING AUTHOR
OF *40 IS THE NEW 80* COMES:**

UNMOTIVATIONAL QUOTES
TO GUIDE YOU NOWHERE

BY: **P.J. STAZ**

Dedication

To my immediate family here on earth
and to those beyond the stars.

Table of Contents

Introduction 1

Unmotivational Quotes 3

Final Message 171

Acknowledgment 172

About the Author 173

Other Titles by P.J. Staz 174

Introduction

Motivational quotes can be confusing because words cannot really motivate an individual, no matter how poetic and true they seem to be when you read them.

Instead, motivation comes from one's own determination, inner energy and strength. Most of the jumbled words you read by self-proclaimed leaders start to sound the same after a while, and most of those quotes are driven by the same idea: believe, work hard, and you too can get a taste of success.

Countless keen and ambitious people have tried to motivate themselves by reading other peoples' leadership advice found in expensive self-help books. Although doing this might provide one with some preliminary and superficial guidance, this approach is inherently wrong for two reasons:

Firstly, the lack of relatability; the type of advice received from a book has little to do with the reader's unique life experiences.

Secondly, if you are simply following someone else's advice and not discovering anything for yourself, how can you expect to be a true leader? You will remain a passive follower, waiting to be spoon-fed opinions and advice that you can repeat at dinner parties to appear more knowledgeable and experienced than you maybe are.

The solution is to get out there and focus on your own life. If you want to be successful, simply do the opposite of what leadership self-proclaimed leaders have done in the past.

Only then will you develop your own style, live your own experiences, and create your own path. Most importantly, you will work towards becoming your best self.

You can do it. This book will help you to achieve success by allowing you to question the conventional wisdom of leaders of the past, whilst taking a comedic and light-hearted approach.

Finally, not every moment in life has to be intense and serious. When faced with challenges or obstacles in life, we often need to stop, take a step back and have a good laugh.

So now is the moment to relax and enjoy these useless quotes that will get you nowhere.

Unmotivational Quotes

Only a few people will taste success,
but you do not have what it takes
to be one of them.

If children are the future,
then we have no hope.

When problems arise, give up and run away.

Starting fires is much easier than
putting them out.

Stepping over others is the best way to
take steps forward in your career.

You can pay someone off to
become a winner.

Finding someone to blame is a skill that
should be learned early.

Look deep into your soul.
You will find that you do not have
what it takes.

If you have failed twice, chances are
you will fail again.

The ambitions of young leaders
should be quashed immediately to
prevent them from bettering
the world.

Peace begins with an argument.

Your leadership style should only depend
on what book is currently popular.

Always aim to do the least
amount of work possible.

Utilize flaws in the system to
your own advantage.

Failure hurts, but you will get over it after
a few beers. Maybe.

Putting your feet up on the table is easier than
putting your nose to the grind.

It takes a big person to know they have lost, so
make sure that you are the smallest person
in the room.

Focus your effort on activities that will get you paid.

Wisdom never paid any bills.

The Universe is a huge place.
There is plenty of
room for errors.

Everyone knows that success
usually happens by accident.

If you are mediocre, just be happy you
have not been fired yet.

Treat others the way you do not want to be treated.

Leadership books will only confuse you;
trade them in for video games
(including this one!).

Always have someone nearby to blame.

Chances are, others will beat you to the punch.

You probably don't have what it takes.
In the face of adversity, drop the task into
someone else's hands.

Stay close to those that fail often.
They make you look better.

Motivate others in the wrong direction.

If you fail to plan, you are planning to fail,
but who really cares anyway?

Ride someone else's wave and
then take credit for their work.

There is no I in the word team,
but there should be.
Because. . .

. . . teamwork has never helped anyone win.

Your chance to succeed has already passed.

Ratting on others will make you feel good.
Try it sometime.

Ignorance keeps us focused.

It is better not to play the game if you know
you are going to fail.
You will save time, money and
embarrassment.

Be the best you cannot be.

Pretending to understand will get
your superiors off your back.

Hard work is easier when you delegate it to
someone else.

Lying is underrated. It is the foundation of
many successful companies.

Crafting an excuse is easier than
facing the truth.

Watching television or cruising the internet
is more educational than reading books.
Futile is resistance.

Using confusing leadership jargon gets your
point across without saying much at all.

[insert motivational leader's name]'s
words should not be trusted.

Offending others makes them
easier to control.

Letting someone else down only hurts
if you did not do it right.

Loyalty can be gained through bribes.

In order to be honest every day,
deny, deny, deny,
then lie, lie, lie.

Taking on challenges is too much effort.
It is best to quit before you start.

Babbling leaders are trying to
make up for their own failures
by making you fail too.
How inspiring!

You can get what you want if you steal
and scam shamelessly.

Question success. Celebrate failure.

Achieving a goal has never helped anyone.

You should always never believe in yourself.

Some say that cutting corners is bad form,
but all that matters is getting the job done
with the least effort possible.

Teach others, but not enough that they will end up
getting a better job than you.

Failure starts with you (and you alone).

Limit your current and future experiences to
maintain a dull intellect.
Life is easier that way.

Honesty and sincerity are what smart people
use as excuses for their failures.

Extra effort rarely makes a difference.

Setting your goals low and achieving them
will lead to a sense of accomplishment.

Quote great minds when you cannot think
of anything else to say.

Pressure feels best when you see it in others.

The quest for greatness starts
with a long nap.

Desire should only guide those
who are unemployed.

The value of striving for greatness should be questioned.
There must be something better to do.

The customer is always wrong.
(Doesn't that feel good to
say for once?)

Futility should be moved to the
front of the dictionary.

Dare to fail. Fail to dare.

Hold goals over the garbage.
When they get heavy,
let them go and forget
about them.

Breaking down barriers is okay as long
as you can put them back up
afterwards to keep others out.

Let someone **else** do it.

Who will be the first to take on a difficult task?
Not I, said the smartest person in the room.

Listening to others takes too much effort.
It is best to just ignore what others say
and go about your day.

Selling out feels good, especially when
you profit from it.

A visionary is someone who can use semantics
to avoid doing any real work.

Only play the game if you know you can win.

Visionaries are usually just lazy people.

Losing often should tell you something.

Nepotism is the most efficient way
to get ahead.

The fountain of knowledge is as useful
as a clogged toilet.

Fake it until you can make it someone
else's responsibility.

If you wake up with drive and determination on your mind,
go back to sleep.

You can catch more bees with honey,
and even more with blackmail.

Be thankful that someone else failed
and it was not you.
You have maintained the façade of
competence for another day.

Do not celebrate the success of your peers;
drown in the misery of realizing you will never
be in their shoes.

Lead by bad example.

Believe in yourself because no one else will.
Maybe do not even do that?

True leadership stems from those who know
how to utilize weak minds to their advantage.

Inspire others to do their worst.

Self-sacrifice is not worth the effort.

Turnover sucks. It gets rid of the people
that make you look good.

Paying attention to detail is not important;
no one is going to notice if you
miss a few steps.

Do not worry about disappointing others.
They will get used to your incompetence.

Never praise; always criticize.

Ego is one of the most underutilized
tools in the business world.

You would be better off with a trash can as a mentor
than a human who claims to be a leader.

When others are showing you how to get t
he job done, let them continue until
they are finished.

Leaders will not accomplish anything without
the willingness to cut corners.

Drive usually leads to accidents.
It is best to just walk.

Powerful words are full of hot air.

Appearing to be a good leader is more effective
than actually **being** one.

Realize, truly realize, that you are failing
in everything you do.

When that little voice says you can't do it,
it is probably telling the truth.

Do not bother searching for the meaning of life
because there is no meaning at all.

Take the easiest job and make it easier.

Quitting is the shortest path to happiness.

Some lead and some follow.
It is best to just follow.

Creating shortcuts will lead to failure quickly,
but at least you won't have to worry
about the problem anymore.

Think without any box. Inside or out.
It is a whole lot easier.

Dissecting problems into smaller pieces
will show you how to avoid them
more easily.

Your morals are only as good as the speed
at which you can dispose of them.

The best way to solve problems is by
not giving people a chance to.

Problems will go away if you ignore them.

Wake up from your dreams; you probably
won't achieve them anyway.

Ask idiots and underachievers for advice.
If you are doing the opposite of them,
you are surely on the right track.

Slacking off is a trait of the best leaders.
They do it undetected with ease.

A true leader knows that they truly know nothing.

Strive to become the best, but only if you
get paid enough to.

Leadership books make great coasters.

Set goals that you have already achieved.
You are guaranteed to succeed again.

If others doubt you, prove them right.

Your chance at success is close to 0.0000005%.

Set the bar high and then
find a way around it.

Nobody will give you anything in life.
You must steal, deceive and lie
to get what you want.

Aim high only when you have to.

Dreaming is unrealistic and pathetic.
You will only become happy once
you realize you will never achieve
your escapist fantasies.

If you have a great mind, do not make it known.
They will only expect more from you.

Going the distance is not worth the effort;
there is always a shortcut.
Pay someone to find it for you.

Eliminate those who are not motivated, and you'll be
left with no one on the planet.

Asking questions not only shows you care;
it also proves that you do not know anything.

Play like a champion another day.

If losing is the best way to learn,
simply do your best to lose.

If you do not do it, somebody else will. Let them.

Since you always have to come down after
climbing a mountain, you might as well save
your energy and stay at the bottom.

Do not worry too hard: you will be replaced
by a robot within five years.

Even when you win, you are still a loser at heart
because you lost many more things before.

Pretending that you've got the job done
is just as good as actually doing it.

The best part of completing a task is
slacking off once you are finished.

Never, never, never do your best.

Be a self-starter who is too lazy to start.

The secret to joy is watching
other people do your work.

Doing the impossible is impossible.
So how can you possibly do something impossible?
It is better to ignore all the philosophical stuff
and just enjoy a day at the park.

You will fail miserably in whatever you do,
no matter how **hard you try.**

No action in our lives is worth anything.

Give a person a fish and they'll eat for a day.
Teach them to fish and they'll leave you alone.

Volunteering would be more
attractive if it were paid.

If your purpose does not help humanity evolve,
do not bother participating in society.

Being #1 means nothing to those
who are bad at math.

Do not involve yourself in a project until it is
almost complete.

Those that tried to do something and failed
should never have tried in the first place.

Visualize yourself as the person
you do not want to be.

No results are better than mediocre results.

A great mind can quickly be attained
using the Internet.

Hope usually leads to disappointment.

Bribes are only bad when they
come in bank transfers.

Follow leaders closely enough that you can
hide in their shadows.

The best open-door policy has a great lock.

Do let people down.

Inefficiency still has the word efficiency in it.

Maximize labor laws that prevent
you from doing work.

Openness and honesty breed weakness.
Selfishness and ignorance build strength.

We learn from mistakes,
so make more of them.

Don't bother shooting for the stars.
They're millions of light-years away;
you'll never reach them.

The truth is only as good as its lies.

The future belongs to those
who live the longest.

Final Message

Now, what should you do with this knowledge?

You only really have two choices: You can embrace these words and work hard to be your worst, or you can ignore each and every word and go accomplish something spectacular.

Whichever path you choose, be cautious about those who drag you down at every opportunity and those who try to walk over you as they embark on their own leadership path. You are responsible for your own life and your own development, and there should be no doubt that you have it in you. Life will be difficult at times, but press on and never keep these words close to your heart.

The only person who can succeed and avoid failure is you. Dig deep inside yourself, find that confidence and use it to the best of your ability.

Once you use your ambition to transform your lazy life into an empowered one, goals will be easier to achieve and you will feel better each day because you are doing something meaningful and fulfilling with your existence.

Since success starts with you, go now and become your best self!

Acknowledgment

Only to the muses that work through us.

About the Author

P.J. Staz is a human being.
He currently resides on
planet earth.

Other Titles by P.J. Staz

Where is the Universe?
A Short Journey to the Furthest Points in Outer Space

◆

40 is the New 80:
A Semi-Practical Guide to the Halftime of Life

◆

Where Are Those Satellites Going?:
A Quick Orbital Adventure of Earth's Selfie Takers

www.ingramcontent.com/pod-product-compliance
Lightning Source LLC
Chambersburg PA
CBHW030311160726
47992CB00005B/1972